THE JPS B'NAI MITZVAH TORAH COMMENTARY

Tetsavveh (Exodus 27:20–30:10)
Haftarah (Ezekiel 43:10–27)

Rabbi Jeffrey K. Salkin

T0339289

The Jewish Publication Society · Philadelphia
University of Nebraska Press · Lincoln

INTRODUCTION

News flash: the most important thing about becoming bar or bat mitzvah isn't the party. Nor is it the presents. Nor even being able to celebrate with your family and friends—as wonderful as those things are. Nor is it even standing before the congregation and reading the prayers of the liturgy—as important as that is.

No, the most important thing about becoming bar or bat mitzvah is sharing Torah with the congregation. And why is that? Because of all Jewish skills, that is the most important one.

Here is what is true about rites of passage: you can tell what a culture values by the tasks it asks its young people to perform on their way to maturity. In American culture, you become responsible for driving, responsible for voting, and yes, responsible for drinking responsibly.

In some cultures, the rite of passage toward maturity includes some kind of trial, or a test of strength. Sometimes, it is a kind of "outward bound" camping adventure. Among the Maasai tribe in Africa, it is traditional for a young person to hunt and kill a lion. In some Hispanic cultures, fifteen year-old girls celebrate the *quinceañera*, which marks their entrance into maturity.

What is Judaism's way of marking maturity? It combines both of these rites of passage: *responsibility* and *test*. You show that you are on your way to becoming a *responsible* Jewish adult through a public *test* of strength and knowledge—reading or chanting Torah, and then teaching it to the congregation.

This is the most important Jewish ritual mitzvah (commandment), and that is how you demonstrate that you are, truly, bar or bat mitzvah—old enough to be responsible for the mitzvot.

What Is Torah?

So, what exactly is the Torah? You probably know this already, but let's review.

The Torah (teaching) consists of "the five books of Moses," sometimes also called the *chumash* (from the Hebrew word *chameish,* which means "five"), or, sometimes, the Greek word Pentateuch (which means "the five teachings").

Here are the five books of the Torah, with their common names and their Hebrew names.

> **Genesis (The beginning), which in Hebrew is Bere'shit (from the first words—"When God began to create").** Bere'shit spans the years from Creation to Joseph's death in Egypt. Many of the Bible's best stories are in Genesis: the creation story itself; Adam and Eve in the Garden of Eden; Cain and Abel; Noah and the Flood; and the tales of the Patriarchs and Matriarchs, Abraham, Isaac, Jacob, Sarah, Rebekah, Rachel, and Leah. It also includes one of the greatest pieces of world literature, the story of Joseph, which is actually the oldest complete novel in history, comprising more than one-quarter of all Genesis.

> **Exodus (Getting out), which in Hebrew is Shemot (These are the names).** Exodus begins with the story of the Israelite slavery in Egypt. It then moves to the rise of Moses as a leader, and the Israelites' liberation from slavery. After the Israelites leave Egypt, they experience the miracle of the parting of the Sea of Reeds (or "Red Sea"); the giving of the Ten Commandments at Mount Sinai; the idolatry of the Golden Calf; and the design and construction of the Tabernacle and of the ark for the original tablets of the law, which our ancestors carried with them in the desert. Exodus also includes various ethical and civil laws, such as "You shall not wrong a stranger or oppress him, for you were strangers in the land of Egypt" (22:20).

> **Leviticus (about the Levites), or, in Hebrew, Va-yikra' (And God called).** It goes into great detail about the kinds of sacrifices that the ancient Israelites brought as offerings; the laws of ritual purity; the animals that were permitted and forbidden for eating (the beginnings of the tradition of kashrut, the Jewish dietary laws); the diagnosis of various skin diseases; the ethical laws of holiness; the ritual calendar of the Jewish year; and various agricultural laws concerning the treatment of the Land of Israel. Leviticus is basically the manual of ancient Judaism.

> **Numbers (because the book begins with the census of the Isra-elites), or, in Hebrew, Be-midbar (In the wilderness).** The book describes the forty years of wandering in the wilderness and the various rebellions against Moses. The constant theme: "Egypt wasn't so bad. Maybe we should go back." The greatest rebellion against Moses was the negative reports of the spies about the Land of Israel, which discouraged the Israelites from wanting to move forward into the land. For that reason, the "wilderness gen-eration" must die off before a new generation can come into ma-turity and finish the journey.

> **Deuteronomy (The repetition of the laws of the Torah), or, in Hebrew, Devarim (The words).** The final book of the Torah is, essentially, Moses's farewell address to the Israelites as they pre-pare to enter the Land of Israel. Here we find various laws that had been previously taught, though sometimes with different wording. Much of Deuteronomy contains laws that will be im-portant to the Israelites as they enter the Land of Israel—laws concerning the establishment of a monarchy and the ethics of warfare. Perhaps the most famous passage from Deuteronomy contains the *Shema*, the declaration of God's unity and unique-ness, and the *Ve-ahavta*, which follows it. Deuteronomy ends with the death of Moses on Mount Nebo as he looks across the Jordan Valley into the land that he will not enter.

Jews read the Torah in sequence—starting with Bere'shit right af-ter Simchat Torah in the autumn, and then finishing Devarim on the following Simchat Torah. Each Torah portion is called a parashah (di-vision; sometimes called a *sidrah*, a place in the order of the Torah reading). The stories go around in a full circle, reminding us that we can always gain more insights and more wisdom from the Torah. This means that if you don't "get" the meaning this year, don't worry—it will come around again.

And What Else? The Haftarah

We read or chant the Torah from the Torah scroll—the most sacred thing that a Jewish community has in its possession. The Torah is written without vowels, and the ability to read it and chant it is part of the challenge and the test.

But there is more to the synagogue reading. Every Torah reading has an accompanying haftarah reading. Haftarah means "conclusion," because there was once a time when the service actually ended with that reading. Some scholars believe that the reading of the haftarah originated at a time when non-Jewish authorities outlawed the reading of the Torah, and the Jews read the haftarah sections instead. In fact, in some synagogues, young people who become bar or bat mitzvah read very little Torah and instead read the entire haftarah portion.

The haftarah portion comes from the Nevi'im, the prophetic books, which are the second part of the Jewish Bible. It is either read or chanted from a Hebrew Bible, or maybe from a booklet or a photocopy.

The ancient sages chose the haftarah passages because their themes reminded them of the words or stories in the Torah text. Sometimes, they chose *haftarah* with special themes in honor of a festival or an upcoming festival.

Not all books in the prophetic section of the Hebrew Bible consist of prophecy. Several are historical. For example:

The book of Joshua tells the story of the conquest and settlement of Israel.

The book of Judges speaks of the period of early tribal rulers who would rise to power, usually for the purpose of uniting the tribes in war against their enemies. Some of these leaders are famous: Deborah, the great prophetess and military leader, and Samson, the biblical strong man.

The books of Samuel start with Samuel, the last judge, and then move to the creation of the Israelite monarchy under Saul and David (approximately 1000 BCE).

The books of Kings tell of the death of King David, the rise of King Solomon, and how the Israelite kingdom split into the Northern Kingdom of Israel and the Southern Kingdom of Judah (approximately 900 BCE).

And then there are the books of the prophets, those spokesmen for God whose words fired the Jewish conscience. Their names are immortal: Isaiah, Jeremiah, Ezekiel, Amos, Hosea, among others.

Someone once said: "There is no evidence of a biblical prophet ever being invited back a second time for dinner." Why? Because the prophets were tough. They had no patience for injustice, apathy, or hypocrisy. No one escaped their criticisms. Here's what they taught:

> God commands the Jews to behave decently toward one another. In fact, God cares more about basic ethics and decency than about ritual behavior.
> God chose the Jews *not* for special privileges, but for special duties to humanity.
> As bad as the Jews sometimes were, there was always the possibility that they would improve their behavior.
> As bad as things might be now, it will not always be that way. Someday, there will be universal justice and peace. Human history is moving forward toward an ultimate conclusion that some call the Messianic Age: a time of universal peace and prosperity for the Jewish people and for all the people of the world.

Your Mission—To Teach Torah to the Congregation

On the day when you become bar or bat mitzvah, you will be reading, or chanting, Torah—in Hebrew. You will be reading, or chanting, the haftarah—in Hebrew. That is the major skill that publicly marks the becoming of bar or bat mitzvah. But, perhaps even more important than that, you need to be able to teach something about the Torah portion, and perhaps the haftarah as well.

And that is where this book comes in. It will be a very valuable resource for you, and your family, in the b'nai mitzvah process.

Here is what you will find in it:

> A brief **summary** of every Torah portion. This is a basic overview of the portion; and, while it might not refer to everything in the Torah portion, it will explain its most important aspects.
> A list of the **major ideas** in the Torah portion. The purpose: to make the Torah portion real, in ways that we can relate to. Every Torah portion contains unique ideas, and when you put all

of those ideas together, you actually come up with a list of Judaism's most important ideas.

> Two ***divrei Torah*** ("words of Torah," or "sermonettes") for each portion. These *divrei Torah* explain significant aspects of the Torah portion in accessible, reader-friendly language. Each *devar Torah* contains references to **traditional** Jewish sources (those that were written before the modern era), as well as **modern** sources and quotes. We have searched, far and wide, to find sources that are unusual, interesting, and not just the "same old stuff" that many people already know about the Torah portion. Why did we include these minisermons in the volume? Not because we want you to simply copy those sermons and pass them off as your own (that would be cheating), though you are free to quote from them. We included them so that you can see what is possible—how you can try to make meaning for yourself out of the words of Torah.

> **Connections:** This is perhaps the most valuable part. It's a list of questions that you can ask yourself, or that others might help you think about—any of which can lead to the creation of your *devar Torah*.

Note: you don't have to like everything that's in a particular Torah portion. Some aren't that loveable. Some are hard to understand; some are about religious practices that people today might find confusing, and even offensive; some contain ideas that we might find totally outmoded.

But this doesn't have to get in the way. After all, most kids spend a lot of time thinking about stories that contain ideas that modern people would find totally bizarre. Any good medieval fantasy story falls into that category.

And we also believe that, if you spend just a little bit of time with those texts, you can begin to understand what the author was trying to say.

This volume goes one step further. Sometimes, the haftarah comes off as a second thought, and no one really thinks about it. We have tried to solve that problem by including a **summary** of each haftarah, and then a mini-sermon on the haftarah. This will help you learn how these sacred words are relevant to today's world, and even to your own life.

All Bible quotations come from the NJPS translation, which is found in the many different editions of the JPS TANAKH; in the Conservative movement's *Etz Hayim: Torah and Commentary;* in the Reform movement's *Torah: A Modern Commentary;* and in other Bible commentaries and study guides.

How Do I Write a *Devar Torah?*

It really is easier than it looks.

There are many ways of thinking about the *devar Torah.* It is, of course, a short sermon on the meaning of the Torah (and, perhaps, the haftarah) portion. It might even be helpful to think of the *devar Torah* as a "book report" on the portion itself.

The most important thing you can know about this sacred task is: *Learn* the words. *Love* the words. Teach people what it could mean to *live* the words.

Here's a basic outline for a *devar Torah:*

"My Torah portion is (name of portion)_____,
   from the book of _____, chapter
_____.

"In my Torah portion, we learn that_____
   (Summary of portion)

"For me, the most important lesson of this Torah portion is (what
   is the best thing in the portion? Take the portion as a whole;
   your *devar Torah* does not have to be only, or specifically, on the
   verses that you are reading).

"As I learned my Torah portion, I found myself wondering:
   ‣ *Raise a question that the Torah portion itself raises.*
   ‣ *"Pick a fight"* with the portion. Argue with it.
   ‣ *Answer a question* that is listed in the "Connections" section of
      each Torah portion.
   ‣ *Suggest a question to your rabbi* that you would want the rabbi
      to answer in his or her own *devar Torah* or sermon.

"I have lived the values of the Torah by _____
(here, you can talk about how the Torah portion relates to your own life. If you have done a mitzvah project, you can talk about that here).

How To Keep It from Being Boring (and You from Being Bored)

Some people just don't like giving traditional speeches. From our perspective, that's really okay. Perhaps you can teach Torah in a different way—one that makes sense to you.

> Write an "open letter" to one of the characters in your Torah portion. "Dear Abraham: I hope that your trip to Canaan was not too hard . . ." "Dear Moses: Were you afraid when you got the Ten Commandments on Mount Sinai? I sure would have been . . ."
> Write a news story about what happens. Imagine yourself to be a television or news reporter. "Residents of neighboring cities were horrified yesterday as the wicked cities of Sodom and Gomorrah were burned to the ground. Some say that God was responsible . . ."
> Write an imaginary interview with a character in your Torah portion.
> Tell the story from the point of view of another character, or a minor character, in the story. For instance, tell the story of the Garden of Eden from the point of view of the serpent. Or the story of the Binding of Isaac from the point of view of the ram, which was substituted for Isaac as a sacrifice. Or perhaps the story of the sale of Joseph from the point of view of his coat, which was stripped off him and dipped in a goat's blood.
> Write a poem about your Torah portion.
> Write a song about your Torah portion.
> Write a play about your Torah portion, and have some friends act it out with you.
> Create a piece of artwork about your Torah portion.

The bottom line is: Make this a joyful experience. Yes—it could even be fun.

The Very Last Thing You Need to Know at This Point

The Torah scroll is written without vowels. Why? Don't *sofrim* (Torah scribes) know the vowels?

Of course they do.

So, why do they leave the vowels out?

One reason is that the Torah came into existence at a time when sages were still arguing about the proper vowels, and the proper pronunciation.

But here is another reason: The Torah text, as we have it today, and as it sits in the scroll, is actually *an unfinished work*. Think of it: the words are just sitting there. Because they have no vowels, it is as if they have no voice.

When we read the Torah publicly, we give voice to the ancient words. And when we find meaning in those ancient words, and we talk about those meanings, those words jump to life. They enter our lives. They make our world deeper and better.

Mazal tov to you, and your family. This is your journey toward Jewish maturity. Love it.

THE TORAH

❖ Tetsavveh: Exodus 27:20–30:10

In the last Torah portion we read about what the Tabernacle was supposed to look like; now let's focus on who is supposed to work in it. Those would be the *kohanim* (priests)—the people in charge of carrying out the rituals, which were mostly sacrifices. Tetsavveh contains detailed descriptions of the special clothing that the High Priest was to wear, and how the priests were to have been inducted into their sacred service to the Jewish people. The portion concludes with a description of the altar for burning incense.

Interesting fact: this is the only Torah portion in Exodus, Leviticus, Numbers, and Deuteronomy that does not mention Moses. This factoid led commentators to imagine that the reading of this Torah portion always coincides with Moses's yahrzeit (the anniversary of his death)—as if the absence of Moses in the portion served as an advance announcement of his death.

Summary

- ▸ The Israelites are to bring beaten olive oil that will be used to kindle the *ner tamid* (the eternal light) in the Tabernacle. (27:20–21)
- ▸ Moses has to bring his brother, Aaron, toward him for induction into the priesthood. The garments that Aaron and his sons are to wear convey dignity and honor. (28:1–3)
- ▸ These special garments include the ephod (a long vest), with a breast piece that was used to determine God's will, a headdress, and a sash. Aaron is to wear bells on the hem of his sacred garment. Both Aaron and his sons are to wear linen breeches—trousers—when they enter the Tent of Meeting or approach the altar. The idea of holy garments survives in the clothing that Catholic priests wear, as well as in what Mormons wear. (28:6–42)
- ▸ There are extensive and distinct procedures that have to be followed in order to consecrate the priests. These procedures include sacrificial offerings. (29:1–44)
- ▸ There are explicit instructions for the construction of an incense altar. The Israelites need incense so that they will not be overcome by the unpleasant odors of animal sacrifice. (30:1–10)

The Big Ideas

> **Judaism relies on continuity from generation to generation.** Just
> as there was a *ner tamid* in the ancient Tabernacle and in the an-
> cient Temples, there is a *ner tamid* in every contemporary syn-
> agogue. This demonstrates the continuity of Jewish tradition
> across thousands of years.

> **Judaism has always recognized different models of religious
> leadership.** Moses and Aaron represent that diversity. Moses is
> the prophet and Aaron is the priest. The prophetic role is to be in
> direct communication with God; the priestly role is to make sure
> that the rituals are correctly observed. Often these roles are in
> conflict, just like Moses was sometimes in conflict with Aaron.

> **Jewish ritual grows and changes, but it always keeps pieces of
> the past.** The priestly garments have never disappeared. They ap-
> pear, in slightly different form, as the "clothing" that is found
> on Torah scrolls. Even the Torah crowns and the bells that adorn
> them remind us of the garments of the priests.

> **Priests can't just jump into doing important work; there needs
> to be an official welcome ceremony.** The Torah requires that the
> priests be ushered into their sacred work with appropriate rituals
> in order to make them, and the Israelites, aware of the presence
> of God in their midst.

> **Judaism is not only God centered; it is also people centered.** The
> practical purpose of the incense in the Tabernacle was to make
> sure that the odor of the sacrifices did not offend the Israelites.
> Jewish ritual must always be concerned with the feelings of the
> people who are involved in it.

Divrei Torah

GOD'S "DRESS CODE"

You probably don't like dress codes that much. Most people don't. But what about uniforms? That's the subject of much of this Torah portion—the special clothing that Aaron and his sons must wear in connection with their priestly duties. The Torah states that the *kohanim* had to wear their special clothing "lest they die." Maybe just their priestly roles would have died—at least for the time being. You may have heard the expression, "Clothing makes the man." The Talmud says something similar with regard to the priests: "When they are wearing their appointed garments, they are priests; when they are not wearing their garments, they are not priests."

There are no more Jewish priests, and the garments that the priests wore are now found only on the Torah scroll. Rabbis and cantors have taken the place of the priests (leading prayers, not sacrifices!). But it is interesting that rabbis and cantors are among the few clergy in the world who don't have to wear special clothing. Some will wear robes or a tallit, but these are customs rather than requirements.

Consider what Catholic priests wear. The Torah's descriptions of Aaron's clothing directly influenced priests' clothing. Some Protestant denominations require their ministers to wear special clothing too, like white collars, when they are performing their pastoral duties. The white robes that some rabbis and cantors wear on the Days of Awe symbolize spiritual purity. But the black robes that some might wear on the Sabbath actually derive from academic robes that professors used to wear, and that faculty and students still wear during graduation exercises. Perhaps rabbis and cantors originally started to wear black robes to emphasize the role of the rabbi as a teacher. Or, maybe the black robes come from the judicial robes that judges wear—to show that rabbis must act with solemn judgment.

We wear uniforms in our own lives. Some schools require uniforms. Sports teams require uniforms. Cheerleading squads require them. Camps have special T-shirts and sweatshirts. The clothing that we wear signifies the crowd that we hang out with, the social class that we inhabit, our tastes in clothing, and even how much money we have. The labels we wear label us as well. And the clothing we wear—and the way we wear it—makes statements about our values and our identity, how we view our bodies and our sexuality.

As Rabbi Sue Levi Elwell writes: "Clothing makes a statement. Are the items you wear mass-produced, or made by hand? Are the laborers who make the garments paid a fair wage? Are you intentionally advertising a company, a brand, a designer, an attitude? Are you declaring your connection to a school, a camp, a community, a philosophy? Are you showing off your prosperity or proclaiming your modesty?"

Clothing matters. Maybe even more than we have ever thought.

A DIVISION OF LABOR

Have you ever noticed that in most synagogues there is a division of labor? Rabbis lead, teach, and counsel. Cantors sing. Jewish educators organize educational programs. Executive directors manage the synagogue. Custodians keep the synagogue clean. While there are many overlaps between these roles (cantors teach and some rabbis sing, for instance), that is the typical system.

The Torah also imagines a sacred division of labor—between the priest and the prophet. Aaron is the first High Priest of the Israelites, and Moses, of course, is the prophet. A midrash says that Moses actually would have wanted to become the High Priest, but God told him to appoint someone else. You can imagine how disappointed Moses was. "God said to him: 'Go and appoint Me a High Priest.' Moses replied: 'Lord of the Universe! From which tribe shall I appoint him?' God replied: 'From the tribe of Levi.' Moses was glad, saying, 'At least he will be from my tribe!'"

The priests were in charge of the rituals of the Jewish people, making sure that the sacrifices were done correctly. The prophets, however, were God's spokespeople, communicating God's will and always emphasizing justice and ethics.

But the differences in their roles go much deeper. The priests had to be from the family of Aaron. It was a hereditary position, like royalty. But prophets did not come from special families. In fact, we barely know the name of Moses's father, and his sons are not important at all. Priests have special clothing. Prophets can wear anything. Priests have to be separate from the people. Prophets live among the people.

But the contrasts are even deeper than that, and those contrasts actually define and shape Judaism. The priest's job was to get the rituals right. Those rituals had to be done correctly, and never change. This was to ensure that life would be stable and constant. The ancient priest would have resonated with the modern cliché: "What is, is." He wants things to *stay the same.*

But the prophet has a bigger vision. She or he doesn't really care that much about getting the rituals right. Their job is to remind people that rituals are worthless unless they are accompanied by acts of justice. They want to change society for the better.

In the words of the Zionist thinker Ahad Ha'Am: "A certain moral idea fills his [the prophet's] whole being. . . . His whole life is spent in fighting for this ideal with all his strength. . . . His gaze is fixed always on what ought to be in accordance with his own convictions."

Judaism needs both the priest and the prophet, because Judaism requires both stability and change. But, in the Torah, which role comes first? Moses becomes a prophet before Aaron becomes the priest.

Yes, ritual is important—but justice and ethics comes first.

Connections

› What uniforms (in all senses of the word) do you wear? How are they significant?

› Our Torah portion contains references to almost all the senses. How do you use your senses in your observance and appreciation of Judaism?

› How would you define a modern-day prophet? Who are some of them?

› Which Jewish role—the priest, who does the rituals, or the prophet, who teaches about righteousness—do you believe to be the most important? Why is this?

THE HAFTARAH

❖ Tetsavveh: Ezekiel 43:10–27

In order to be a Jew, you need a good imagination. And that is pre-
cisely what the prophet Ezekiel has. This week's Torah portion ends
with a description of the incense altar that will be used in the ancient
Tabernacle (*mishkan*). Generations later, the prophet Ezekiel has accompanied his people into exile in Babylonia, and he imagines aloud
what the someday-to-be-rebuilt Temple in Jerusalem will look like.

But before he tells them about that grand plan, he must get them to
repent of the sins that forced them to go into exile in the first place.
Ezekiel mixes hope and responsibility.

The Vision Thing

The prophet Ezekiel, writing from exile in Babylonia, has a vision of
how the rebuilt Temple will look, focusing on the altar. This makes
sense because the altar, where sacrifices will be offered, is certainly
a central place in the Temple. But he makes something very clear: he
will only tell the exiled Judeans about the Temple's design after they
have acknowledged their sins. Because Ezekiel, like the other prophets, believed that it was those sins that got them into Babylon in the
first place. The siddur (prayer book) agrees with this, reminding Jewish worshipers: "Because of our sins, we were exiled from our land."

If sins could result in exile from the land, sins could also lead to
the destruction of Judea and the First Temple in Jerusalem. Which
sins were responsible for these? Take your pick. The Mishnah says,
"It was because of idol worship, prohibited sexual relations, bloodshed, and neglect of the agricultural sabbatical year." We can understand the first three. Idolatry means worshiping other gods. Prohibited
sexual relations destroy the fabric of the family. Bloodshed is, well,
bloodshed—destroying the very image of God within every human
being. But the Mishnah goes one step further: neglecting the sabbat-

ical year of the land, refusing to let the land lie fallow for one year in seven—disrespecting the Land of Israel and, with it, the earth itself.

But wait. There's more. It's written in the Talmud, "Jerusalem was destroyed only because they desecrated the Sabbath," . . . "only because they neglected reading the *Shema,* morning and evening," . . . "only because they neglected the education of school children." These are religious failings, though we might also think that the punishment—destruction and exile—doesn't fit the crime. And here is another: "Jerusalem was destroyed only because the small and the great were made equal." This means that there was no longer any authority in the land. We're no longer talking about religious issues now; we are talking about what happens in a society that falls into anarchy.

But if there is to be a real reason for exile, this quote from the Talmud might be it. "Because there was baseless hatred." Simply put: the Jews hated each other for no particular reason, and could not get along—and, for that reason, destruction resulted. To which Rabbi Abraham Isaac Kook, the first chief rabbi of prestate Israel, replies: "There is no such thing as 'baseless love.' Why baseless? This other person is a Jew, and I am obligated to honor him. There is only 'baseless hatred'—but 'baseless love'? No!" Hatred without cause will tear apart a society, and this internal weakness will make it vulnerable. The obligation to love our fellow human, on the other hand, confers a strong and caring society that is much more cohesive and strong, able to withstand external challenges.

Here is another Talmudic teaching, in the form of a legend about the destruction of Judea and the First Temple: "When the First Temple was about to be destroyed, bands of young priests took the keys of the Temple and mounted the roof of the Temple and exclaimed: 'Master of the Universe, we did a bad job guarding the Temple. We are returning the keys to you.' They then threw the keys up toward heaven. And the figure of a hand emerged, and took the keys from them."

Perhaps God still has the keys to the ancient Temple. Perhaps it is time for modern Jews to ask God: "Can we have the keys back? We are ready to practice Judaism even better than our ancestors did. We are ready to let go of hate and let love prevail." Wouldn't that be a wonderful vision?

❖ Notes

❖ Notes

CPSIA information can be obtained
at www.ICGtesting.com
Printed in the USA
LVHW08s0951050818
585984LV00004B/434/P